Careers

written by

Wendy Benger

KAEDEN ♥ BOOKS™

Title: Careers
Copyright © 2013 Kaeden Corporation
Author: Wendy Benger
Photography and Design: Signature Design

ISBN: 978-1-61181-431-6

Published by:
 Kaeden Corporation
 P.O. Box 16190
 Rocky River, Ohio 44116
 1-800-890-READ(7323)
 www.kaeden.com

Printed in Guangzhou, China
NOR/0913/CA21301680

First edition 2007
Second edition 2013

Table of Contents

Mr. Brown's class was talking about **careers** in the **community**. Mr. Brown said, "We will make a list of your parents' careers."

Sara's dad drives a school bus.

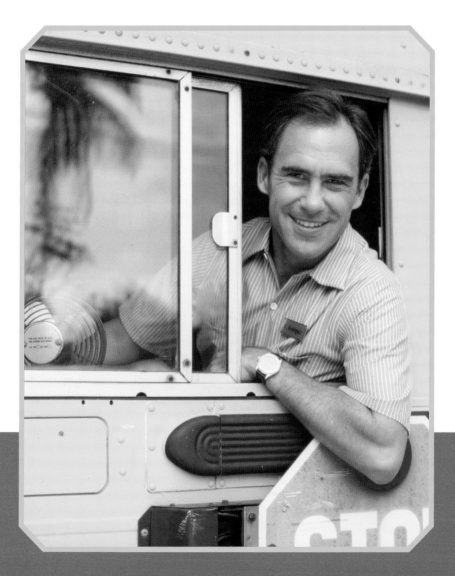

Martin's mom and Carla's dad **teach** children.

Anna's dad puts out fires.

helmet

air tank

face mask

protective gloves

Firefighters wear a self-contained breathing apparatus (SCBA) so they can breathe in smoke filled environments.

Fred's mom and Grace's mom take care of young children.

Jen's dad **treats** sick children.

A doctor who specializes
in treating children
and babies is called a
pediatrician.

Maria's dad takes care of teeth.

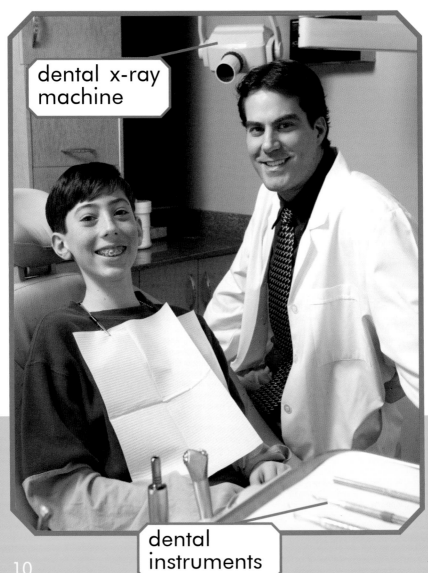

dental x-ray machine

dental instruments

Kate's mom helps sick people.

ear thermometer

nurse

Jessica's mom fixes cars.

Robby's dad cuts hair.

Jackie's mom sews clothes.

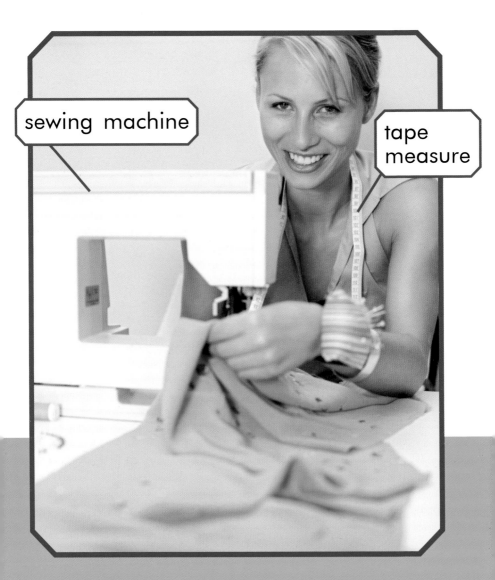

sewing machine

tape measure

Dan's dad builds houses.

Will's mom **designs** buildings.

architectural model

Josie's dad paints houses.

Liz's dad bakes cakes.

Mike's mom cooks pizzas.

Pete's mom types **letters**.

The class read the whole list together.

bus driver
teacher
firefighter
childcare worker
doctor
dentist
nurse
mechanic

hair stylist
seamstress
builder
architect
painter
baker
cook
executive assistant

What career would you like to have?

Glossary

career - an occupation or profession

community - a group whose members live in a specific area, share government and often have a common heritage

designs - prepares the sketches or plans for a new structure

letter - a written or printed form of communication

teach - to impart knowledge of or give instruction in

treats - to deal with in order to relieve or cure

Index

24